Arth

WIC

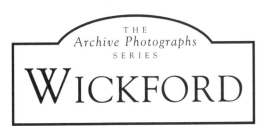

THE
Archive Photographs
SERIES

WICKFORD

The parade of shops on Hall's Corner built with locally made bricks from the Nevendon Road Brickworks in 1930. In the foreground of the picture is a bed of horseradish.

An aerial view of Wickford taken around 1950 showing Nevendon Road recreation ground before Chaplin Lodge was built. On that site was a large war time shelter partly underground which could rarely be used as it was flooded most of the time. On the opposite side of the road was an Italian P.O.W. Camp and in later years two of the huts were used as the Clinic.

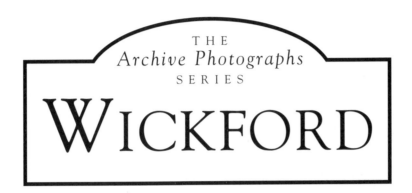

THE
Archive Photographs
SERIES

WICKFORD

Compiled by
Peter Hall

CHALFORD

First published 1996
Copyright © Peter Hall, 1996

The Chalford Publishing Company
St Mary's Mill, Chalford,
Stroud, Gloucestershire, GL6 8NX

ISBN 0 7524 0354 0

Typesetting and origination by
The Chalford Publishing Company
Printed in Great Britain by
Redwood Books, Trowbridge

This aerial view shows the High Street north to south and the crossroads at Halls Corner.

Contents

Wickford Railway station before it was modernised. The signal box has now been demolished.

Introduction

Some years ago, when an old Aunt of mine died, I was given a box of negatives and, after printing them up, I realised I could put together a history of Wickford. This sparked off a lot of interest and over the past three years I have visited various clubs and functions and local schools with my slide show. I have always been received by very attentive audiences, many of whom ask if I had ever thought of putting my pictures and knowledge into a book. This I have now achieved. Being a true Wickfordian, whose family can be traced back to the early 1800s, I was given a lot of help and first-hand information and I hope this book will prove to be both interesting and worthwhile.

Wickford (Wykeford, Wygeford, of Wicfort) is named from its situation at the ford of the Crouch, in a hollow between Billericay and Rayleigh. While Stone, Bronze, Iron Age and Roman remains have been found in the area, a village of this name existed by the time of King Edward the Confessor. Wickford began to grow in the Victorian years. The soil was rich and loamy and the main crops were wheat, oats and small amounts of beans, barley, peas and turnips. The agricultural depression certainly affected Wickford and gradually agricultural land fell into disuse. Although in 1848 the majority of Wickford's population were engaged in labouring on the land, the town had grocers, butchers, bricklayers, a plumber and painter, a milliner and dressmaker, an ironfounder and smith, a vet and two doctors. By 1863 there were saddlers, wheelwrights, a cattle dealer and even a straw hat maker. At the turn of the century Wickford still had a very rural appearance with an abundance of elm trees and it was possible to pick a bunch of wild flowers as you walked the length of the High Street. Without doubt the coming of the railway was the catalyst for Wickford's change from agricultural village to commuter town.

The proximity of the railway opened up the market for the local nurseries. H. Spencer & Son, Irvon Hill (1911) grew flowers and tomato plants specifically for sale in the Stratford market. The greenhouses, belonging to Mr Cork, also in Irvon Hill, were always full of grapes, cucumbers and tomatoes. Children of the village took time off from school for pea picking during June.

At the beginning of the twentieth century, the Parish Council seemed anxious to sell off the agricultural land of the village in plots. The building rush did benefit some local people; the Carter family, resident in the village from the eighteenth century at least, had the chance to build a large number of properties and the Wickford brick works provided bricks for the local market. Another of the oldest business names in Wickford is that of Darby, an agricultural business established in 1862, which was enlarged some 40 years later by the invention of the famous Darby Digger machine.

The education of children in Wickford was, until 1861, in private hands, but National Schools began to be built around the country from the middle of the nineteenth century. The one in Wickford was built in Southend Road on the corner of Mount Road and could accommodate 75 children.

A Wickford Chronology

975 First mention of Wickford in the Will of Aethelflaed, one time landowner.

1086 At the time of the Domesday Book, Wickford had a population of about 150.

1154 Wickford Church given to Prittlewell Priory.

1811 Congregational Chapel built in Runwell Road.

1823 It was planned to make a ship or barge canal from the Crouch going towards Billericay; nothing became of it because the water supply would be unreliable.

1832 Wickford became a post town.

1851 A survey was taken in Wickford just before the Crimean War when there were just 490 people living in the village. In 1901 the figure had reached only 638.

1887 Wickford had a postmark which was J.48.

1887 The railway came to Wickford (goods traffic). Passenger service opened on January 1 1889 with one daily train to London.

1888 Wickford Cricket Club formed - yearly subscription 2/6d.

1898 Barclays Bank opened every Monday for $1\frac{1}{2}$ hours only.

1899 The streets were first lit by spirit lamps donated by local business people.

1901 In 1900 the village well dried up and by January 1901 Southend Waterworks Company were promoting a Bill in Parliament to supply water to the area and Wickford became interested in obtaining a supply from this company.

1902 A stretch of path in the High Street was kerbed and tarred.

1905 Roads were becoming more frequently used by cyclists.

1906 The growth of the population meant that sewage disposal became a problem. Although there was a man who could empty cesspits halfway up for 2/6d and right out for 4/-, this method of disposal was unsuitable for an area with a growing population. In January 1906, notices were served on owners who lived within 100 yards of the sewer requiring them to connect their premises to the system. One of the first houses to be connected to the sewer was Bridge House and the Brickfield cottages were connected soon after it was in working order.

1908 Telephone service provided.

1914 The new County Council school was opened in Market Road which is now the present Infants School.

1914 The first Fire Brigade.

1914 Tennis was being played in the village regularly.

1914 Formation of the branch of the Boy Scouts.

1914 There was a 12 miles per hour speed limit in Wickford High Street.

1917 A refuse collection became available in the area.

1920 First police station.

1921 Population now 1,475.

1923 Electricity came to Wickford.

1926 A manual telephone exchange was set up.

1937 Wickford County Senior School, now the Junior School, in Market Road, was built.

1955/56 Building of the Hanningfield reservoir.

1956 Electrification of the railway.

1972 Bromfords School opened.

1972 Market moved to its present site.

1973 Willowdale opened.

1982 Ladygate Centre opened.

1988 Rebuilding of Halls corner (Ladygate phase II).

1988 Replacement of old railway bridge after 101 years.

One
A Walk Through the High Street

The south end of Wickford High Street around 1920. Graylins was a general grocery shop and the other cottages became shops in later years - a sweet shop, a shoe repair shop and a fruit and vegetable shop.

A gathering outside the old blacksmith's shop on Halls Corner. It is not only horses waiting to be shod!

Upson's blacksmiths and saddlers shop on Halls Corner.

A picture of the High Street looking north, late 1920s.

Hall's Corner as it was in 1904. Previously known as Forge Corner, it shows Upsons, one of the villages's blacksmiths. The corrugated shed belonged to H.E. King, the Greengrocer.

An old cottage in Wickford High Street at the turn of the century on a site next to where Woolworths is today.

J.D. Prentice & Son, a family business of cycle engineers for over 100 years, originally from Manor Park. They moved from the cottage home and workshop in the middle of the High Street (the present site of Woolworths) to corner premises at London Road.

Wickford Street.

Another view looking north towards the Broadway, c. 1910. the elm tree marks the entrance to the village doctor's house, now the site of a gentlemen's outfitters.

A view of the High Street at the turn of the century looking towards the Broadway.

This large house in the middle of the High Street was the residence of Doctor John Marshall who practiced for 48 years in Wickford. A front was added and it is now a gentlemen's outfitters.

Suttons old shop which opened in the High Street in 1941.

The thatched cottage next to shops in the High Street is built on the site where Woolworths stands today. R. True was the local tallyman - he rode round the district on his trade bicycle selling his wares.

Mrs. Dudley's sweet shop - every child's favourite - next door to the cinema. This is now the site of the High Street's newsagents.

The Carlton cinema in the High Street opened its doors for entertainment in 1936 - workmen are seen putting the finishing touches to its name. During the Second World War it had to be camouflaged to cover the bright white walls. The cinema was closed in the late 1950s and was converted into what is now Woolworths.

The cover of the Carlton cinema programme.

The High Street as it looked in the 1930s. The house on the left was called 'Rylands' and was the first home of Dr C. Campbell. Later it was the house where Mr Cochran, the dentist, lived.

The High Street as it looked around 1934/35. The parade of shops on the right of the picture were built with bricks from the Nevendon Road brickworks. Next door to Willcocks, the shoe shop, was Mr. Culley's fancy shop where you could purchase newspapers, magazines, toys and gift. A wireless and repair shop came next where for the price of sixpence you could get the accumulator recharged.

Two views of the Congregational Chapel (above from 1900, below in 1960) built in the High Street opposite Market Road in 1875, after the chapel built in Runwell Road in 1811 developed wet rot and foundation troubles due to frequent flooding. Fifty people could be seated in the balcony of the new chapel and 300 on the ground floor and it had a very nice organ. Unfortunately, due to redevelopment of the town centre, it was demolished early 1970 and a new chapel was built around 1973 on the Ladygate site.

Wickford Chapel.

The five-bar gate next to the Congregational chapel in the High Street was the entrance to the Great Eastern Railway's reservoir built in 1907; the water was diverted from the River Crouch to be pumped up to the steam engines. The horse and cart on the opposite side of the road was owned by Reddingtons of Pitsea and is making a delivery of lemonade to a cafe around 1908. The weather-boarded cottages are now the site of the Woolwich Building Society.

These old weatherboard cottages in the High Street seen in 1904 stood on the site where Willowdale is today. One of the village pumps can be seen with the white painted fence around it; water could be purchased at a halfpenny a bucket.

W. Waide Pollard & Sons Ltd stood on the corner of Market Road on the site of a general grocers shop run by Mr and Mrs Halls. They moved to their present site in 1972.

Another of the weatherboard cottages housed R. Jephson's saddler and harness making business. He also mended the local lads' football cases.

G. May boot maker situated on the High Street side of the railway bridge.

An advertisement from a 1915 parish
magazine for the Boot and Shoe Stores.

Cramphorns corn chandlers shop in the centre of the High Street early 1930s. Next door was a small stationers and tucked in beside the shops were two private residences.

In 1950 Wickford had a town clock which could be seen outside the wireless shop in the High Street.

The Nevendon Road bridge as it was before 1935 when it was replaced. Croft House on the right was also built with local yellow stock bricks in 1924 - it is now a public house called The Duke.

Building the new bridge in Nevendon Road in 1935 as the old one was not suitable for the increasing motor traffic.

Residential properety in the south end of the High Street in the late 1920s.

Some 50 years later - 'Ladybrow', the home and surgery of Dr. Frew, is still in the High Street but it was soon to be demolished for the entrance to the Ladygate Centre.

Two shops in the High Street, late 1950s, opposite what is now Ladygate Centre.

Mr. Sidney Hall standing in the doorway of the old shop 1930.

Looking from the High Street towards the old Nevendon Road Bridge, c. 1930. All the houses were built with local yellow stock bricks and are still standing today.

The start of the building of Christ Church in 1973.

This aerial picture, taken in the late 1960s, shows the back of the shops on Halls Corner. 'Ladybrow', the doctor's house has been demolished and the site cleared ready for the development of Ladygate shopping complex.

Shops at the end of High Street and the pair of villas which were demolished in the 1970s to make way for the by-pass.

A not too busy High Street, c. 1960. Fine Fair supermarket stands back on the left.

Pages garage, car body repair shop in Market Road on the site where Barclays Bank stands today.

High Street shops opposite Market Road, c. 1970. Westway travel agents is the only one remaining.

Looking from the High Street under the railway bridge towards the Broadway, c. 1900. The shoe shop of G. May is on the left.

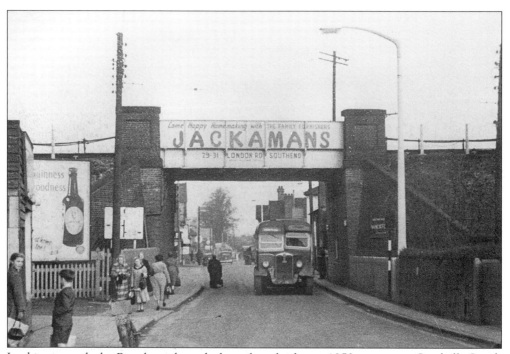

Looking towards the Broadway through the railway bridge, c. 1950, one sees a Cambells Coach on its run to Pitsea.

Two
The Broadway

This photo was taken from the railway bridge looking towards Runwell, c. 1970.

Just through the railway bridge into the Broadway was the Wickford fruit shop which later became the Cigar Box. The two men with the horse and cart were brothers who owned and ran a coal merchants and haulage business in the village.

A view of the Castle Inn taken in 1900.

Sitting on his motorcycle outside the
Cigar Box is Mr Cork who later owned the
Nurseries in Irvon Hill.

A view looking towards Runwell with the Castle Inn on the right. Notice the cobble stones at
the bottom of the approach road to Great Eastern Railway station.

Mayes Bros., the ironmongers - a very busy family business in the Broadway from 1910 to 1960.

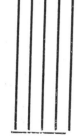

An advertisement taken from an old parish magazine showing the varied assortment of the goods they stocked.

Ruffhead was the landlord of the Castle Inn and his son ran the Jobmaster traps and landaus business. This picture was taken around 1924.

One of the local police constables with some of the villagers standing at the bottom of Station Approach, c. 1920. The Castle Inn is on the right.

The weatherboard cottage on the left of the picture next to the Castle Inn was pulled down to be replaced by a red brick house in 1910.

Looking towards Runwell from outside Mayes Bros. shop, c. 1912.

On this early picture of the Broadway there is no kerb on the left hand side of the road. Kerbing started around 1901 and it took about four years to complete around most of the main roads. George English's drapers shop is on the right; the building is still standing today.

This view of Southend Road corner was taken around 1860 and shows the White Swan public house sign on the left of the picture opposite Franklins the family butchers.

Two pictures taken of the same area in the Broadway but some 30 years apart. Pardey & Johnsons was a general grocers store and off licence and the village post office in the 1950s.

1826. Wickford. Essex.

At the Broadway end of the High Street, the row of shops with the blinds down were all owned by the Gigney family. A coal merchants and haulage business was run from the big house at the end of the picture.

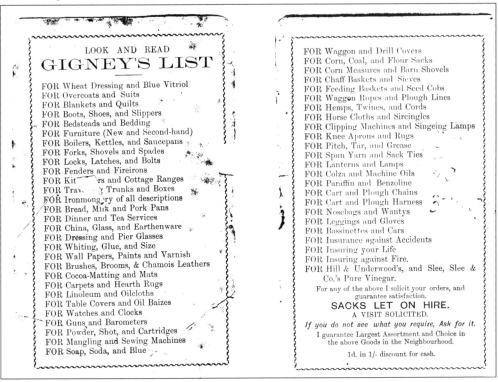

LOOK AND READ
GIGNEY'S LIST

FOR Wheat Dressing and Blue Vitriol
FOR Overcoats and Suits
FOR Blankets and Quilts
FOR Boots, Shoes, and Slippers
FOR Bedsteads and Bedding
FOR Furniture (New and Second-hand)
FOR Boilers, Kettles, and Saucepans
FOR Forks, Shovels and Spades
FOR Locks, Latches, and Bolts
FOR Fenders and Fireirons
FOR Kitchers and Cottage Ranges
FOR Travelly Trunks and Boxes
FOR Ironmongery of all descriptions
FOR Bread, Milk and Pork Pans
FOR Dinner and Tea Services
FOR China, Glass, and Earthenware
FOR Dressing and Pier Glasses
FOR Whiting, Glue, and Size
FOR Wall Papers, Paints and Varnish
FOR Brushes, Brooms, & Chamois Leathers
FOR Cocoa-Matting and Mats
FOR Carpets and Hearth Rugs
FOR Linoleum and Oilcloths
FOR Table Covers and Oil Baizes
FOR Watches and Clocks
FOR Guns and Barometers
FOR Powder, Shot, and Cartridges
FOR Mangling and Sewing Machines
FOR Soap, Soda, and Blue

FOR Waggon and Drill Covers
FOR Corn, Coal, and Flour Sacks
FOR Corn Measures and Barn Shovels
FOR Chaff Baskets and Sieves
FOR Feeding Baskets and Seed Cobs
FOR Waggon Ropes and Plough Lines
FOR Hemps, Twines, and Cords
FOR Horse Cloths and Sircingles
FOR Clipping Machines and Singeing Lamps
FOR Knee Aprons and Rugs
FOR Pitch, Tar, and Grease
FOR Spun Yarn and Sack Ties
FOR Lanterns and Lamps
FOR Colza and Machine Oils
FOR Paraffin and Benzoline
FOR Cart and Plough Chains
FOR Cart and Plough Harness
FOR Nosebags and Wantys
FOR Leggings and Gloves
FOR Bassinettes and Cars
FOR Insurance against Accidents
FOR Insuring your Life
FOR Insuring against Fire.
FOR Hill & Underwood's, and Slee, Slee & Co.'s Pure Vinegar.

For any of the above I solicit your orders, and guarantee satisfaction.
SACKS LET ON HIRE.
A VISIT SOLICITED.
If you do not see what you require, Ask for it.
I guarantee Largest Assortment and Choice in the above Goods in the Neighbourhood.

1d. in 1/- discount for cash.

A list of wares which could be bought at Gigney's Stores, copied from an original railway timetable of 1894.

Franklins -family butchers 1800 to 1960. They attended the cattle market in Chelmsford, Rochford and Wickford to buy the animals which were then driven home to Wickford where they were eventually slaughtered in the slaughter house at the rear of the shop. Renowned for home produced brawns and 'lovely sausages'!!

Standing in the doorway of the White Swan public house as it looked around 1890, is Mr Edward Cox, the landlord. There were stables at the rear of the property and the piece of land in the front of the picture was known as the Green. It was around 1880 when the White Swan first opened.

Two pictures of celebrations outside the White Swan.

This row of red brick terraced villas was built around 1900 in the Broadway. Over the years they were all converted into shops. Mr Jordan, a watchmaker, was the first coloured resident in Wickford.

The Broadway around 1920.

Old Victorian villas in Runwell Road, known as Wickford Place, which were demolished during the sixties to make way for a new parade of shops.

Colonel Kemble leading the hunt through the Broadway towards Runwell fields in the early 1920s. Colonel Kemble lived in Runwell Hall and played a dominant role in village affairs. He unfurled the Union Jack on Empire Day at celebrations at the village school and also audited the Parish magazine accounts.

A view of the Broadway taken in the early 1950s.

A view of the Broadway, c. 1960.

Three

Swan Lane Area and Market Day

Six little maidens playing in the water outside Victoria Villas in Swan Lane around 1913.

Looking up Swan Lane - the row of villas were built at the end of the nineteenth century.

A cottage standing on the corner of Swan Lane.

Swan Lane in the 1950s.

THE "SWAN" INN,
WICKFORD.
(Now fully Licensed).

CHOICEST WINES & SPIRITS,

DINNERS & TEAS provided on the shortest notice.

FIRST-CLASS STABLING AND LOOSE BOXES.

Horses, Traps, Broughams, and Wagonettes,

On hire at moderate charges.

TRAINS MET at the STATION

Proprietor   -   -   -   R. W. PATMORE

The Swan Inn advertisements.

First World War soldiers in Jersey Gardens. '

The same location many years later.

A picture taken from a postcard, dated 1924, of villas in Jersey Gardens.

This weatherboard cottage is to be found in Swan Lane on the corner by Jersey Gardens.

The Wickford Public Hall at the junction of Elm Road and Jersey Gardens opened as a Community Hall in 1908. The 'Welcome Home Celebrations' for the forces returning to Wickford from the First World War were held here. It has been the venue for many public functions - dances and cinema after the Carlton closed - but there were many complaints that when it rained hard the sound was marred by the fact that it had a tin roof. More recently it had been used as a gymnasium.

The Public Hall, Jersey Gardens - getting ready for the welcoming home celebrations for the returning forces of Wickford. Twenty nine members of the armed forces from Wickford lost their lives in the First World War.

Elm Road looking towards Swan Lane, c. 1900. There were many great elm trees in the area in the nineteenth century.

The site of the old market opposite the Castle Inn around 1918. In 1922 it moved to a new site where Willowdale is today.

Stage coaches journeying from Southend to Romford stop at The Castle Inn. This picture, taken in the early 1900s from the railway embankment, also shows the cattle market opposite The Castle Inn.

A view of the old market taken from the railway bank around 1969 showing the corrugated leantos used for the stalls. Ashes and clinker from the local hospital were put on the ground but if it was not available cockle shells from Leigh cockle sheds were used; the town then smelt somewhat like the seaside. The market moved to its present site in 1972.

Market day in Wickford was Monday. Two pictures of the market taken from the railway embankment, early 1920s. This is now the site of Willowdale.

Above and below: Rodd & Slipper's small and large animal markets in Market Road.

Four
Runwell Road

An old thatched cottage in Runwell Road known as Guinea Pig Hall which was once the residence of the Rector of the Congregational chapel. On the other side of the road was the chapel cemetery and in the direction of the High Street was a row of weather-boarded cottages called Chapel Row.

BIG FIRE AT WICKFORD, EXTENSIVE DAMAGE IN EARLY MORNING BLAZE, TWO BUSINESSES INVOLVED. A fierce fire that spread with amazing rapidity occurred early on Thursday morning in the business centre of Wickford. It caused the complete destruction of Messrs H.C. Harvey and Son's haulage contractors' and coal merchants' business premises at the Broadway, together with Mr. H.C. Harvey's residence, and seriously affected the adjoining buildings of Messrs Darby and Company, agricultural and motor engineers, Runwell Road. Reliable sources place the damage at not far short of £10,000. The fire apparently started in a small stable containing a quantity of straw in Swan Lane, adjoining the rear of Messrs. Harvey's property, but in no way associated therewith. An article in the *Southend Pictorial Telegraph* from April 29, 1939.

A scene in Runwell Road around 1912 showing Stileman's estate on the left. The house on the right of the picture was called Orchard House and the meadow beside it was where one of the local butchers kept his cattle and sheep until they were ready for slaughter. Milk deliveries were by cart from churns.

Stileman's - a large timber-boarded house in the area of Runwell Road next to the cricket ground. The name probably originated from a fifteenth-century Wickford landowner, William Styleman. Darby's business moved here from Russell Gardens and became known as Stileman's Works.

Runwell Garages in the early 1970s (Note the price of a gallon of petrol).

Next to Guinea Pig Hall was the weather-boarded cottage and the builders yard of Frank Carter.

RUNWELL CHURCH.

Above and below: pictures copied from 1921 postcards. The tower of Runwell church is fifteenth century but the round columns of the arcades are from a church which was a place of pilgrimage in Thomas Becket's day. Legends, superstitions and reports of ghostly goings-on have combined to give Runwell the reputation of being one of the most haunted places in the county. St. Mary's church is said to have no less than five ghosts and probably more. A deeply cut claw-like mark on the south door of the church is said to have been made as the devil tried to make his exit from the church in pusuit of a corrupt priest in the sixteenth century.

A view towards Church End Lane corner showing the old school house.

With Good Wishes for Xmas and the New Year

from Runwell Rectory.

Copied from a Christmas card dated 1919.

Looking towards the Quart Pot around the turn of the century - the old rectory brick wall is on the right.

Looking up Runwell Road just past the Quart Pot in the late 1800s.

The Quart Pot as it was in the late nineteenth century. Originally a residential house, it later became a public house and in 1924 the Salvation Army used a private room at the back for meetings and would leave their paper, The War Cry, in the hollow oak tree for the followers to take and read.

A picture of the same public house but taken some years later.

Five

Southend Road

A 'finger post sign' stands in the middle of a patch called the Green at Southend Road corner next to the bridge as it was before 1915. It was under this old oil lamp on The Green where the Salvation Army would meet and sing on a Sunday.

This picture was taken from the rear of The Castle Inn looking across at the old Southend Road bridge around 1910.

Looking back towards the bridge and the Broadway end of the High Street from Southend Road. The high ground on the right hand side of the picture was to enable pedestrians to walk up the Southend Road when it was flooded.

The opening ceremony of the new bridge for Southend Road, 1915. There is a bronze plaque inserted in the brickwork on the left hand side of the bridge as you go up Southend Road.

A gathering of people at the opening ceremony of the Memorial Nurses Home in Southend Road around 1920. It was built as a war memorial to the twenty-nine members of the armed forces who lost their lives in the First World War.

Wickford War Memorial Nurses Home in Southend Road before its demolition.

The Auction Rooms in Lower Southend Road were next door to the Midland Bank and opposite the old post office. They later became the Three Day Woodshop.

A parade of small shops in Lower Southend Road, locally known as 'Shanty Town', consisted of a cafe, gentlemens' hairdressers, cycle repair shop, mens' clothes shop, auction rooms and a bank.

The Methodist church in Southend Road was built 1927 and demolished in 1984.

A very rural looking Southend Road with no major buildings between the bridge and the School. It is a very different picture today. Franklin's fields on the left is now a housing estate and a road leads off to one of the local doctor's surgery.

The thatched cottage at the corner of Mount Road that became the Church of England School.

On January 10 1908 it was destroyed by fire.

The Fire Brigade at Chelmsford was sent for but as the telegram did not have a signature it was not clear who would pay the brigade's expenses so they would not turn out and the Billericay Fire Brigade came. It was a horse drawn manual engine and at Crays Hill the children came from a nearby school to help push the engine up the hill but on hearing that the engine was going to Wickford School they withdrew their support and went back to classes. By the time Brigade arrived there was nothing left but the brick walls and some window frames. It is not clear how the fire started. It may have been a spark from the chimney or oily rags thrown onto the fire after cleaning the oil lamps used for lighting.

The school was rebuilt on the site while the children resumed lessons in a temporary classsroom made available to them by Mr Ruffhead of the Castle Hotel. The school reopened in November 1908.

Not a house in sight! A very rural view of Wick Lane at the end of the nineteenth century.

A view of Edward Farr's engineering works taken from the air in 1954.

Wick Lane looking towards the railway crossing. Railway cottages and the Crossing Keeper's cottage can be seen on the right of the picture.

A steam train approaches the crossing at Wick Lane.

A bit of rough road! Russell Gardens before it was made up. It now leads to the industrial estate.

A 1950s view across Russell Gardens and the back of Crompton Terrace, the houses built by Darby for his key workers. The railway track is the main Southend to London line.

A pen and ink drawing of St. Catherines church, Wickford, c.1875. The history of the church dates as far back as the thirteenth and fourteenth century when a church was first erected on the site. The two bells were cast in 1460 and the octagonal font is also fifteenth century.

In 1876 the present St. Catherines church was completed, replacing the old church which stood on the same site and had become both dilapidated and inadequate. Copied from a picture dated 1923.

The old farmhouse of Shotgate Farm which was sold by auction in August 1891. It still has the old pump dating back to 1872.

Wickford Hall, an old nineteenth-century manor house, standing at the rear of St. Catherines church and now converted into flats.

The propeller marks the spot where two aeroplanes collided at Shotgate on 7 March 1918. Both pilots perished in the crash. Captain A.B. Kynock was buried at Golders Green and Captain Henry Clifford Stroud in a small military section at Rochford Parish Church. The inscription reads: This spot is sacred to the memory of Capt. H. Clifford Stroud killed in action at midnight on 7 March 1918. Faithful unto Death. The propeller is of the modern metal controllable-pitch type, complete with spinner, and presumably the old wooden 1918-type propeller must have rotted away.

An aerial view of Wickford taken May 1985 looking across the main Southend to London railway line to the roundabout and surrounding roads.

76

Six
London Road

Ivy Cottage.

'Ryelands', built at the end of the High Street in 1937 for Dr Campbell. It was a doctor's residence and surgery until 1976 when the Basildon Council bought it and made it into a home for homeless people, building an extension on the end of it. It is now the local offices for the Basildon Council.

A pair of old cottages from the early 1900s which stood on the corner of Woodland Road facing the main London Road. They were demolished in the 1960s, making way for shops which have had many changes of use.

A view up London Road. The trees on the right of the picture are where the police station is today.

Cottages on the corner of London Road opposite St Andrews Church in the 1920s.

The Mission Room, which is now known as the small hall, was built in 1901 in the London Road. In 1935, to cope with a still expanding population, St Andrews was built next to the Mission Room. But in 1963 this dual-purpose building was replaced by a permanent church which was dedicated on 30 November 1964.

The nissen hut on the left hand side of the picture is where the fire station used to be before it moved into the present site in Nevendon Road in 1960.

Old villas in London Road which are now a vets and the Wickford Press.

The Wickford Gospel Hall used for religious meetings, c.1925. It was demolished in the early 1990s.

This house in the London Road was a home for nursing mothers in the late 1920s.

The old Milestones Hut - the Catholics' place of worship some years ago. An old map shows the site of the church was once reserved for St Bartholomew's Hospital for an annex to the London hospital if needed. Land for a new church was purchased in 1925 but the church was not built until 1951. The existing church of Our Lady of Good Council officially opened in 1972.

Bridge House Farm was a seventeenth century house built on a 194-acre site in London Road. It played a big part in the development of the town. Almond Avenue, The Chase, Deirdrie Avenue and Bridge House Close were all built on land which once belonged to the house as was the Catholic church in London Road. It was sold for demolition and the building of Bridge House Close which provided another 22 houses. The remaining land went to form part of the recreation ground in Nevendon Road.

Just over the river, the old villas in London Road around the turn of the century.

Looking down Castleton Road towards the river bridge which had a raised walk-way for the use of pedestrians when the river was in flood.

St Margarets church, Downham, parts of which date back to the thirteenth century. A fire destroyed parts of the church, which have since been rebuilt, on March 28, 1977.

Seven
Nevendon

The Peculiar Peoples chapel in Nevendon Road around 1920.

The old Nevendon Road bridge looking towards the Peculiar Peoples chapel early 1900s.

The old Nevendon Road bridge looking towards the High Street around 1920 before Croft House (now The Duke) and the three terraced houses were built.

A peaceful walk down Wick Drive before any development started.

A rural summer scene looking at Elder Avenue as it was the early 1960s. Red and grey squirrels and rabbits were often seen.

North Crescent School with the bypass and garage at the top of the picture.

Brickfield Cottages, Nevendon Road, built for the workers. The brickworks made yellow stocks and reds which were used to build Runwell Hospital, The Duke public house, Halls Corner, Wick Drive, lots of shops in the High Street, the post office in Southend Road and parts of Chartwell, the home of Sir Winston Churchill.

Tye Corner, Nevendon Road, changed to make way for the new by-pass.

In 1950 this was a general store - it is now an Indian restaurant.

Bromfords Farm, Nevendon Road was damaged by a V2 rocket during the Second World War.

A cottage on the corner of Borwick Lane and Nevendon Road -now a very busy main road to Basildon and the A127.

Eight

The Railway
Comes to Wickford

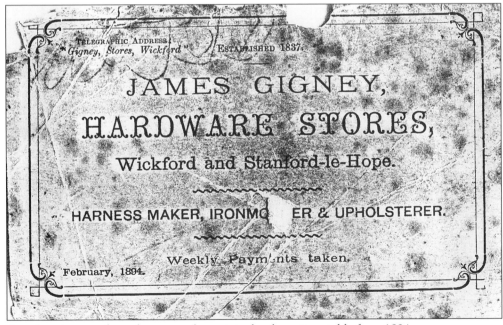

An advertisement from the cover of an original railway time-table from 1894.

A train pulls in to Wickford station. The Great Eastern Railway came to Wickford in 1887 and, before the station was rebuilt in 1980, there was a foundation stone on the outside of the building stating this fact which had been laid by the Rev Beresford Harris, Rector of Runwell. The station put Wickford on the map. Farmers could begin to think of making profits again as the railways enabled quicker distribution of produce. Before the railway, goods such as coal, seed potatoes, peatmoss and cattle came first to Battlesbridge by barge and were then transported to their final destination. Construction of the line entailed building a large embankment and a bridge in Wickford which meant several buildings had to be destroyed. A line for goods traffic opened in 1888 and a passenger service followed on January 1889. There was a turntable which enabled the steam trains to be turned around for the return journey and also a large goods yard. The line was extended to Southminster in 1889 for goods traffic and Wickford station became known as Wickford Junction. It was now easier to get to London and as rural properties were cheaper than in the London area the Wickford population grew. In 1907 a reservoir was built in the town. It was located on the site of the existing car park and held over two million gallons of water, taken from the River Crouch, which was used by the steam trains.

G.E.R. engine standing in Wickford station and the station staff of the day.

A train pulls out of Wickford station bound for Southend. The viaduct and lock gates can be seen in the bottom left-hand corner of the picture.

In February 1988, for just a few hours after 101 years service, Wickford was once again without a railway bridge spanning the High Street.

The old bridge was replaced by two new sections each weighing 31 tons.

Nine
The Darby Digger

Sidney Darby

Thomas Churchman Darby was a nineteenth-century farmer who lived at Pleshey and started the Darby Agricultural Engineering Company. In 1858, at the age of 17, he patented a horse-hoe. Some of these hoes were actually still in use eighty years later. In 1877 he produced the first Darby Digger which was a steam digging mechanism. Various inventions are attributed to the Darby family: an 8' 3" plough; a beet lifter; tractor wheels; mole drains and a reaping machine were all designed by Thomas Churchman Darby. Screw Diggers, manufactured in 1895, was attached to a traction engine and the digging forks were replaced by a horizontal, rotating mechanism. These were exported to many parts of the world. The Darby inventions proved of interest to the royal family. At the Royal Show in 1913 the late Mr Thomas Albert Darby, eldest son of Mr Thomas Churchman Darby, the inventor, demonstrated the digger to King George V. The family moved to Russell Gardens in 1900 where he could build workshops and he even built a row of cottages to house workmen. He later moved to premises in Runwell Road, the site of Stilemans old manor house and grounds.

Sidney Darby was the son of Thomas Churchman Darby. He carried on the old traditions and received many awards for his inventions. His vans covered the district carrying out farmers' repairs. He stocked wearing parts of all machinery, from cardboard milk-bottle stoppers, through milking machines and ploughshares, to the combine harvester. He died in 1962. The Darby Digger lives on in Wickford as, on August 10, 1993, Charrington Taverns opened a new public house in Radwinter Avenue bearing the name.

These two pictures show groups of workers outside the Darby works and stores in 1918.

From left to right: Bill Lepper, Sidney Darby, Stanley Nichols, Mr Blair, Will Gowrers, Mr Dodds, Mr Tornton, Alf Carter, Mr Young.

Two of the Darby inventions.

The premises of S.C. Darby (Wickford) Ltd were gutted by fire in May 1966. There were fears of the fire spreading to the Runwell Garage petrol pumps opposite when the teleraph poles and wires caught alight.

Ten

The Floods, Riverworks and the By-Pass

A view of Halls corner as seen from the bedroom window of my neighbour's house on Saturday morning, 6 September 1958. The landing craft by the side of the bus was loaned by Messrs Carter & Ward. The black mark on the side wall of the end house shows the level the water reached during its peak.

Reflections of the floods of 1958. Croft House in the High Street was built in the early 1920s when it was a residential home enjoying views over green pastures. It is now a public house called The Duke which looks out on to the Wick Estate and the Wickford Relief Road.

The passengers were marooned all night on the top deck of this bus on Halls corner.

The empty bus after the passengers had spent all night on the top deck.

104

The lock gates which were built at the rear of the High Street on land which is now the Council car park, to divert water from the river into the reservoir for the use of steam trains.

A NIGHT TO REMEMBER

September 5, 1958 brought chaos as Wickford suffered one of the worst floods in the history of the town. The statistics of this storm are impressive: 3.27 inches of rain fell in 90 minutes in Wickford and an area of 724 square miles had over two inches of water. People who experienced it will never forget. In the early hours of the evening a torrential cloudburst hit the town which sent water rushing down the Southend, Runwell, and London Roads meeting up at Halls corner, the lowest part of the town where the water reached a level of six feet. Approaches to the town were completely cut off and the muddy water swirled into houses and shops causing many thousands of pounds worth of damage. Cars were abandoned and sixteen people were marooned all night on the top deck of a double decker bus which came to a standstill on Halls corner.

Opposite: 'The morning after the night before' - September 6, 1958. Two aerial pictures showing the extent of the flood water at Halls corner.

Halls corner.

Pushing his way through the water on Southend Road corner.

The landing craft comes to the aid of people in Wick Drive.

Sergeant Adams, the policeman of the day.

One of the boats brought in from Lake Meadows, Billericay, put to use in Runwell Road.

A picture taken from the Nevendon Road bridge in 1960 when the course of the river was altered to solve the flooding problems.

Looking towards the railway and the stretch of river at the Southend Road end.

Land at the rear of Croft House, now The Duke public house, to be included in the making of the new road.

In August 1976, work began on a new by-pass road which had been spoken about for many years to take heavy traffic away from the High Street. In August 1979 the new road was opened by County Highway Chief, David Fisher.

Looking towards Christ Church shows the transformation from green pastures as a bridge is erected over the River Crouch and a roundabout built.

Aerial view showing the roundabout , the supermarket and the Council carpark in the centre of Wickford.

110

Eleven

Local Organisations

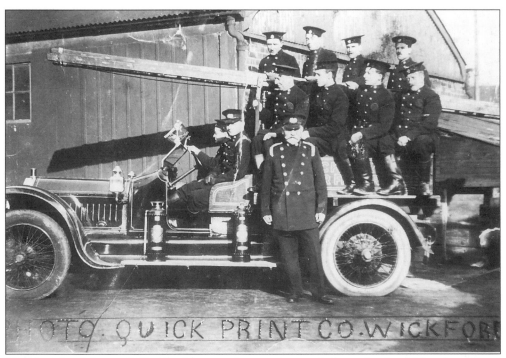

Wickford fire fighters, 1929. The Minerva fire engine once belonged to Lord Hamilton. Some of the men on the engine are Albert Lovell, Alf Fairey, Percy Windsor, Broad, Draper, Joe Tilbury, Captain Plantin. The picture was taken in the yard at the Castle Inn.

Members of Wickford's Fire Brigade with their appliance in London Road. Back row, left to right: Bert Barker, -?-, ? Stollery. Front row: Alf Fairey, Bob Wright, Bill Thompson, Ben Coote, Joe Tilbury, Frank Halls.

At the turn of the century, Wickford's fire fighting force consisted of businessmen on a part time basis. In 1914 their appliance was a ladder on a hand drawn trolley kept in a shed on the opposite side of the road to Halls corner. Volunteers were called out by flares and later by messengers on bicycles. In 1939 the fire service moved into the London Road premises and they then had two full time firemen and their first purpose-built engine had arrived - a Dennis. In 1952 they acquired another more up-to-date Dennis appliance. In 1960, when they moved to their station in Nevendon Road, they had a new Bedford T.K. with a Rolls Royce engine which could carry approximately 400 gallons of water.

Wickford's Fire Station opposite Halls Corner at the beginning of the Second World War.

Wickford's Fire Service appliance at the beginning of the war in the station in London Road opposite the existing police station.

Mobile first aiders.

Special constables.

The Homeguard.

The Red Cross and the A.R.P.

Wickford Branch of the Girls' Brigade.

The 1474 Squadron of the Air Training Corps was formed in Wickford in 1941.

Twelve

People and Events

Spectators outside the pavilion at Wickford Cricket Club.

Wickford Cricket Club Cricket Week, 1932. Back row, left to right: A.G. Mayes, G.F. Bird, K. Mayes, R.W. Patmore, P.E. Block, R.C.R. Vanderzee, W. Timson. Second row: H. Silverstone, S.D. Gibbs, S. Mapleson, W. Cawthorn, C. Salmon. Front row: M.H. Kelly, A.J. Kershaw, E. Bottom.

Wickford Rovers F.C. 1923-24. Back row, left to right: H. Clampin, S. Carter, G. Wallace, H. Flowers Esq. (President), F. Block, W. Fish, W. Debenham (Captain). Front row: J. Clutterbuck, J. Gear, P. Block, N. Palmer, F. Obec.

The Wickford mixed hockey team, 1950. Back row, left to right: Ted Cox, Lois Nissim, Wally Haddon, Roger Foley, Stan Coates, Major Giles, Chick Thomas. Second row: Pearl Haddon, Winnie Coates. Front row: Mary Gooch, Stella Metcalfe, Beryl Spencer.

Mr Robert Hall takes some of his workers on a day's outing to Newmarket.

Dancing the maypole at the British Legion Carnival Fete, 1935.

Childrens' decorated cycles and prams at the Jubilee Carnival and Fete, 1935.

The Coronation Queen of 1937, Miss Muriel Stephens, and her Maids of Honour, the Misses Molly Deacon, Eileen Barclay, Enid McFadden and Enid Joslin together with the Rev Munson and the Rev Potter.

Wet coronation celebrations, May 12 1937. A scene outside The White Swan public house, taken from a window in Franklin's, the butchers house.

An armistice parade on the cricket field in Runwell Road, 1919.

Another Armistice Parade crossing the road to go into the Carlton Cinema in 1946.

Two policemen to the day -
Constable Bolden and Constable
Drane.

'A pen'orth of chips to grease your lips' -
a favourite phrase of Mr Bill Ely when
you visited his fish and chip shop on the
corner of Market Road, now the
chemists.

V.E. Day celebration - two pictures of a street party in Wick Drive, Wickford.

Express Dairy, Woolshots Farm. The van driver is Mr Jack Humphries.

Motor landaulette on hire from R. W. Patmore, 'The Swan', Wickford.

Gigneys Van.

English the butchers. Hubert English drives his van while his brother W.L. English stands at the front.

Halls of Wickford with their pedal-powered deliveries as it was in the 1940s.

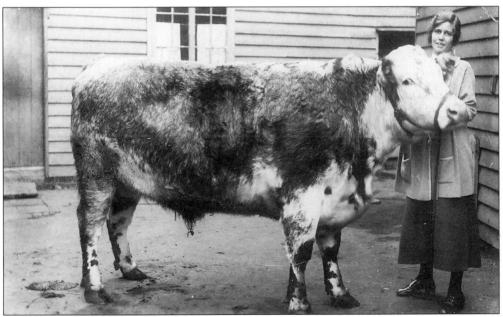

Miss Edith Franklin in the yard of the butchers shop with one of the prize bulls.

Acknowledgements

My thanks go to all those people who kindly lent photographs or postcards that have been included in this book. Mention should also be made of photographs and newspaper cuttings collected by my late Mother, Mrs. A.M. Hall which provided a useful record.

This early 1970s view of the High Street was taken from the railway bridge. It shows what progress has been made in the redevelopment of Wickford since that date.